An Hachette UK Company
www.hachette.co.uk

First published in Great Britain in 2015 by Ticktock,
an imprint of Octopus Publishing Group Ltd
Carmelite House, 50 Victoria Embankment
London, EC4Y 0DZ
www.octopusbooks.co.uk
www.ticktockbooks.co.uk

ISBN 978 1 78325 224 4

A CIP record for this book is available from the British Library.
Printed and bound in China
3 5 7 9 10 8 6 4 2

Written by Mandy Archer  Designed by Doch & Doris Design and Development Ltd
Creative Director: Miranda Snow  Managing Editor: Karen Rigden
Production Controller: John Casey

Picture Credits
Every effort has been made to trace the copyright holders, and we apologise in advance for any unintentional omissions.
We would be pleased to insert the appropriate acknowledgement in any subsequent edition of this publication.

istockphoto.com  alvarez 57 br: Fenne 10 al: happyborder 10 cl: jenek222 13 bl: Liliboas 70 m: lilul3 24 m:
Mat Hayward 18 cl: photopix 15 m

Shutterstock  Amber Williams 53 br: AnetaPics 12 cl, 37 bl, 40 b: Annette Shaff 20 l, 64 bc, 75 c, 77 br: ANP 75 b cl: Antonio
Gravante 9 al, 64 ar: Cheryl E. Davis 62 cr, chloe7992 56 bl: Christopher P. Bamber 64 br: cynoclub 38 bl, 39 bl: dezi 4 m, 5 m:
Dusan Po 10 cr: Elena Dijour 64 bl: Eric Isselee 20 cr, 22 bl, 23 bl, 30 l, 30 r, 31 l, 31 r, 45 bl, 56 r, 57 bl, 66 ar, 66 bc, 74 cr,
74 bc, 74 br, 75 a, 78 ar: Erik Lam 21 bc, 45 br, 47 a, 56 al, 57 al, 57 ar: Ermolaev Alexander 17 l, 53 bc, 53 bl, 67 br: GlOck 78 br:
Grisha Bruev 14 m: Helga Esteb 53 ar: HelleM 49 al: iadams 63 c: iko 42 m: IrinaK 67 cl: Ivonne Wierink 1 m: Janelle Lugge 43 m: Javier
Brosch 29 br, 38 ar, 75 bc, 75 bl: Joca de Jong 10 r: JStaley401 10 ar, 61 m, 71 m: Karramba Production 6 cl: Khoroshunova Olga
34 m: Ksenia Raykova 6 ar: Larry Maurer 12 al: lenetstan 21 ar: Lenkadan 13 bc: Lex-art 77 bl: Lilia Beck 7 ar: Liliya Kulianionak 6 br: 51
m: 65 bl: Linn Currie 25 m: Mat Hayward 7 cr, 13 ac, 65 al: Mila Atkovska 7 al: Monika Wisniewska 12 bl: Morten Normann Almeland 8 a:
natrot 62 br: Nikolai Pozdeev 19 br: npine 66 c: Paul Matthew Photography 18 br, 32 a: Pavel Hlystov 17 r: PCHT 10 bl, 49 bl: Phil Date
38 al, 39 al: Photobac 45 ar: pixshots 33 br: poutnik 48 a: PozitivStudija 35 m: Raisa Kanareva 18 ar: rebeccaashworth 36 ar, 36 bl:
Rita Kochmarjova 37 al, 60 m, 64 al, 65 ar: Robynrg 21 br, 38 cl, 38 br, 67 ar: RoJo Images 68 cr, 69 ar, 69 bl: Scott Bolster 10 br:
Soloviova Liudmyla 65 ac: stepmorem 65 bc: Subbotina Anna 39 cl: Susan Schmitz 20 cl: tobkatrina 53 ac: Utekhina Anna 20 r: verca
65 br: Viorel Sima 7 bl, 39 ar, 80 br: Vitaly Titov & Maria Sidelnikova 26 a, 26 ar, 26 cr, 26 br, 29 bl: Vivienstock 48 b: Vlad Ageshin
49 br: VladisChern 55 br: Volkova 29 ar: Volodymyr Burdiak 13 al: Waldemar Dabrowski 64 ac: WilleeCole Photography 19 ar, 22 ar,
31 al, 39 br, 41 b, 74 bl, 75 cl: WitthayaP 22 al: Zaretska Olga 75 cr

Thinkstock  Dorottya@Mathe 3 bc: Mark Herreid 37 cr: Adam Edwards 76 br: adogslifephoto 41 a: Brian McEntire 40 a: c-foto 44
bl: cynoclub 17 cl, 21 ac, 32 ar, 33 al, 76 ar: DAJ 77 ar: Dixi© 44 br: Ed Phillips 17 cr: Eric Isselee 32 bl, 32 br, 33 al: feedough 44 al:
geargodz 27 ar, 27 ac, 27 bc, 27 br: GlobalP 28 ar, 28 bl, 29 c, 46 ar, 62 ar, 74 al, 74 ac: Ingram Publishing 76 bl:
John Mcallister 74 ar: Jupiterimages 29 al: Katrina Brown 12 cr: Liza Barry 50 m: lucato 78 bl: Mapoula 9 br: monels 76 al:
nickpo 8 bl: Purestock 9 bl: ronibgood56 77 al: Silense 32 al, 44 ar, timaj 33 cr, 47 b: WesAbrams 78 al:
WilleeCole 29 bc, 33 ar, 45 al, 74 al: YekoPhotoStudio 28 al

# Totally Cute Puppies

## Contents

# Too Cute!

Who let the dogs out?

# CHAPTER 1

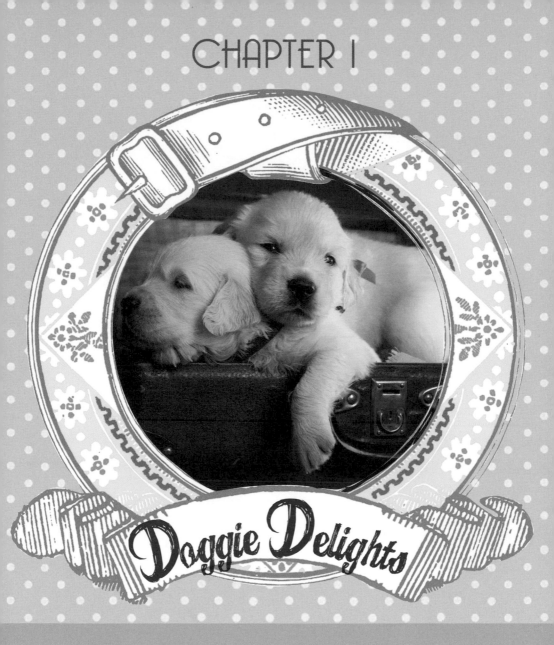

Doggie Delights

Are you potty about puppies? From the poshest pedigree to the messiest mutt in the park, pups are furry, friendly and up for fun! Whether you're a proud pet owner or your head is full of doggy daydreams, your animal adventure starts here...

# Barking Brilliant!

## What makes a dog such a special pet?

They are man's best friend. Dogs are sociable animals that soon become devoted to their owners. The newspapers and Internet are full of stories of pups making heroic rescues to save people.

*1*

*2*

No matter where you've been or what you've done, your dog will always be pleased to see you when you come home. It's impossible to look at a pup's waggy tail and not smile!

*3* Puppies and dogs come in all kinds of wonderful shapes and sizes. Every breed has its own unique colouring, features and characteristics.

Living with a doggy keeps us cheerful. Research has officially proved that people with pet pups are happier than those without.

*4*

Dogs can sniff out all kinds of yummy and yucky smells. Inside their noses there are an incredible 220 million scent cells. Some dogs, like beagles, have many more.

Pups are super-playful! They can't help rolling in muddy puddles, chewing socks and running after balls.

Many dogs have jobs. Some help blind people, while others are trained by the police to track scents. Other breeds work on farms rounding up sheep.

They also go bananas at the sight of a lead or the sound word of the word 'walkies'!

Dogs keep you safe. Most will try and guard their home, barking loudly at the first sign of trouble.

They're family. Dogs like to live in packs – your pet sees those living in your house as the other members of his pack. This is what makes him so loving, loyal and keen to hang out with you 24/7.

# Pawfect Pooches

What's your top dog? There are so many breeds to choose from!
Colour in the paw print next to the pup that you would love to stroke.

## Pomeranian

A cute toy dog with
a full ruff of hair
around its neck. Its fur
grows in all sorts of
colours, from creamy
white to blue-black.

## West Highland
## White Terrier

Lively pup with a
thick coat of fur, little
legs and bags of
personality. Perky ears,
white beard and a
wet button nose.

# Beagle

Long ears, big eyes and a dappled coat – it has to be a beagle! Its wiry fur keeps off brambles when it runs through bushes and ferns.

# Golden Retriever

Warm-hearted, blonde pup that's chocolate box cute! A lovable pet with a face that actually seems to smile when you walk into the room.

# Great Dane

Gentle-hearted puppy that grows very, very big! Short, silky fur, enormous paws and a long tail that tapers to a point.

# Mixed breed

Not every pup has to be a pedigree! Dogs that are a mixture of different breeds are just as beautiful.

# Magical Mix-ups

Hybrid dogs are a cross between two different breeds.
Every one is unique and these new pups also have fabulous name
mash-ups! Labradoodles, puggles and cockerpoos!

## Mix and match!

Can you work out these delightful doggy combinations?
Draw a line to match each name to the correct pedigree parents.

1. Maltese Terrier and Yorkshire Terrier — E

A. Schnoodle ✓

2. Golden Retriever and Collie — F

B. Pugapoo ✓

3. Springer Spaniel and Cocker Spaniel — D

C. Puggle ✓

4. Pug and Beagle — C

D. Sprocker ✓

5. Schnauzer and Poodle — a

E. Morki ✓

6. Pug and Poodle — B

F. Golli ✓

Check your answers on page 80.

10

Can you dream up a brand new doggy combination? Draw a picture of the adorable little pup, then write its official name underneath.

by ................................................

# At Your Service...

As well as being loyal, friendly and impossibly cute, dogs are hard workers! Many pups have special skills and can be trained to follow signals and commands.

## Search and rescue dog

The first search dogs are thought to have been St Bernards - a huge mastiff breed from Switzerland. Nowadays many different types help rescue travellers that are lost or injured. They also do vital work seeking out survivors in disaster zones after events such as earthquakes and avalanches.

## Sheepdog

Not many farms can operate without a sheepdog in residence! Herding dogs like Border Collies are smart pups that can understand complex whistles and commands. They work with the farmer to expertly round up sheep and cattle.

## Police dog

The most common police dogs are German Shepherds - intelligent, brave animals that are strong enough to pin down a suspect. Some forces prize their K-9s so highly they give them their own police badges and IDs.

## Sleigh dog

Huskies and other sleigh dogs are an important form of transport in snowy Arctic regions. They work in teams to pull sleds loaded with passengers, post and supplies. Well-trained packs also make brilliant racers. Mush! Mush!

## Guide dog

All across the world, thousands of guide dogs are working hard to help blind people live a normal life. Guide dogs are picked as very young pups and trained carefully so that they stay steady, calm and loyal to their handler at all times.

## Sniffer dog

Sniffer dogs are excellent at detection. The police use them to hunt out criminals, explosives and illegal substances. As well as having an amazing sense of smell, bloodhounds are born with a natural tracking instinct.

## Other waggie workers

- Acting dog
- Hearing dog
- War dog
- Therapy dog

# !Too Cute!

Yep. A hug would be good right now.

# CHAPTER 2

## Puppy Patrol

A pup is a friend that needs love and care forever, just like you!
It only takes a little thought and effort every day to make a pet feel
safe and content. How would you welcome a new puppy?

# My Puppy Promise

Are you ready to make your puppy promise? Think carefully about what it means to be a good dog owner. If you're truly ready to be there for your furry best friend, read the pledge and sign your name at the bottom.

I promise to be kind to puppies everywhere. If I am lucky enough to have a dog come to live with me. I will give it all of the things that it needs to keep its tail wagging. Every puppy needs...

- a cosy bed
- good food
- fresh water
- walks every day
- lots of cuddles

I will do all that I can to make sure that my pup's coat stays shiny. its eyes stay smiley and its nose stays cold and wet!

Signed ___Olivia Mitchell___

Write your name here.

Choosing a name for a new pup is a big decision. Will you go for something cute, funny or unusual? Read the choosing tips, then write in a name for the marvellous mutts below.

# Look and listen

When it comes to picking a name, you might just need to look at your pup. Does it have fluffy fur, a cheeky face or a dappled coat? Your pet can be a great source of inspiration!

~~Curly~~

Scamp

Patches

# Keep things simple

Pups respond best to short, high frequency sounds because they find them easiest to hear. Think about names that begin with consonants, taking care to avoid anything that could be confused with a command.

~~Beau~~

~~Molly~~

Jasper

# Don't forget

Once you've decided, you will be using your dog's name a lot. Shorter names are much easier to shout when you need to call your pup back quickly.

~~Stella~~

Kyla

Cody

# My fave names

Curly.....    .Beau....    Stella......    Molly....

# Four Furry Feet

Some puppies are sweet and shy, others are bold and barky!
Every dog is different, so when you meet a new one take the time
to watch it for a while first to see how it likes to be treated.

## Feeling shy

Always check with an adult before touching any dog that you don't know, as nervous pups can nip. If the pup seems unsure, help it feel relaxed by getting down on the floor alongside it and avoid eye contact so the puppy doesn't feel threatened.

## Heavy lifting

If your pup wants to be picked up, scoop it up gently by placing your arms around its four legs and bringing it towards you. Hold the puppy close to your chest. It's your way of saying, "relax buddy, I've got you!"

## Patted pooch

Gently stroke your pup from its head down to its tail, running your hand in the direction of the fur. Many dogs love having their ears rubbed and their tummy tickled, too.

# Canine Couture

When you've really got to know your puppy, you can start having fun together! Many owners like to dress up their pets. If you decide to give it a try, always make sure that your dog is safe and comfortable.

## Dress-up rules!

**1** Ask an adult before you start and choose a costume that allows your pet to move freely and go to the toilet if they need to.

**2** Check that your puppy can see and hear properly in their costume and that there are no parts that they could chew and swallow.

**3** Don't put your pet in anything that will make them overheat.

**4** Only keep your puppy dressed up for a short amount of time. Don't let them roam outside with clothes on, as they could get their outfit caught.

**5** Reward your pet with lots of treats for being a star. If they don't seem comfortable, however, take the costume off straightaway.

*What do you think? Too much?*

# Cutie Quiz

What type of puppy are you? Take this quiz and you might discover that some people and pooches have a lot in common!

1. Your favourite movies are...

A. cute chick flick ☐

B. daft comedies ☐

C. action-packed adventures ☐

D. heart-warming animal tales ✓

2. When you get to school, you head to...

A. the cloakroom to check your hair ☐

B. the canteen to find your friends ✓

C. the playground to play ball ☐

D. the classroom to chill out ☐

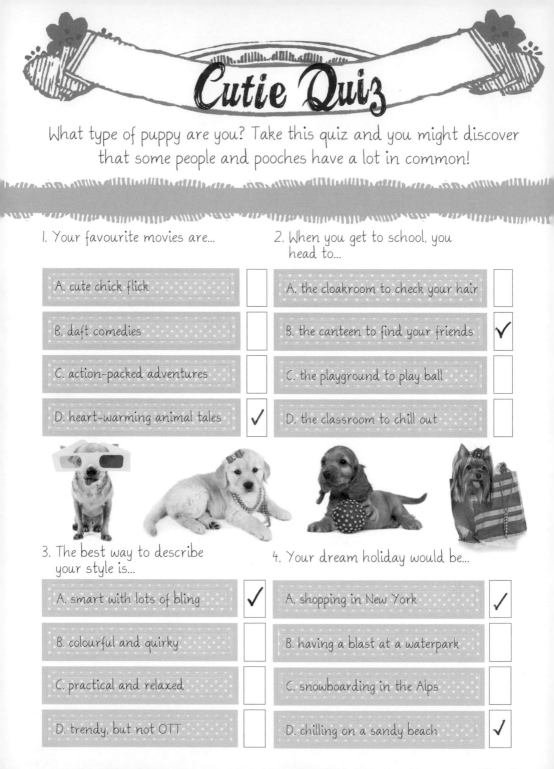

3. The best way to describe your style is...

A. smart with lots of bling ✓

B. colourful and quirky ☐

C. practical and relaxed ☐

D. trendy, but not OTT ☐

4. Your dream holiday would be...

A. shopping in New York ✓

B. having a blast at a waterpark ☐

C. snowboarding in the Alps ☐

D. chilling on a sandy beach ✓

**5. Your family always complain that you...**

| | |
|---|---|
| A. hog the bathroom | |
| B. talk over the telly | |
| C. jump on the sofa | |
| D. take ages to get out of bed | ✓ |

**6. The motto that most suits you is...**

| | |
|---|---|
| A. think big, dream bigger | |
| B. a smile makes everything better | |
| C. where there's a will there's a way | |
| D. tomorrow is another day | ✓ |

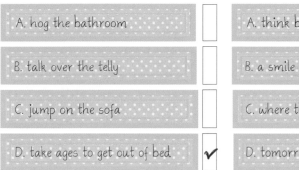

# Mostly A s - pampered Pekingese

You're fluffy, fashionable and always well-groomed, just like the adorable Pekingese. When they need some pedigree pampering, your friends know just who to call!

# Mostly B's - jolly Jack Russell

Have you ever played with a Jack Russell Terrier? You should get along well - you're both playful, happy and full of fun. It seems you've got a habit of turning frowns upside down!

# Mostly C's - spirited Spaniel

Wow - you struggle to sit still for a minute! Cocker Spaniels are just the same. You are both bouncy, excitable and always on the go. If only everyone had as much energy as you do!

# Mostly D's - mellow Mastiff

You're so laid-back, you're almost horizontal! You think the same way as a Mastiff. Why rush today what could be done tomorrow, when you could take it easy instead?

# Ages and Stages

Are doggy ages the same as ours? Do puppies teethe, play and learn, just like babies? Let's take a peep at those adorable baby days.

## Hello world!

A mother dog normally gives birth to a litter of up to six puppies, but she could have as many as a dozen. At first, puppies have their eyes shut. They nestle into their mum to feed and keep warm.

## Waking up

After a couple of weeks, most new puppies will begin to open their eyes. Their ears open up, too. Little by little, the dogs start becoming aware of the world around them.

## Eating and growing

After a month, puppies start developing teeth. A healthy young dog has a big appetite, needing at least four meals a day to grow big and strong.

## First steps

By three weeks, pups will be able to walk, make yapping sounds and wag their tails. Things suddenly start to move very quickly. Once they are mobile, puppies want to get out and explore!

## Leaving the nest

Puppies aren't ready to join a new human family until at least six to eight weeks old. Up until then, they need to be near mum. As well as feeding them milk, she teaches them precious lessons about life in a pack. Now that they're ready to move on, pups are full of energy and curiosity, although they still need lots of naptime, too.

# It's a Dog's Life

Dogs and puppies age at a different speed to humans. Most dogs are thought to be mature by the age of seven years old. Look at the chart to find out how old your pet is in doggy years.

## How old?

| Human Years | Small Dog Years | Medium Dog Years | Large Dog Years |
|---|---|---|---|
| 1 | 15 | 15 | 15 |
| 2 | 24 | 24 | 24 |
| 3 | 28 | 28 | 28 |
| 4 | 32 | 32 | 32 |
| 5 | 36 | 36 | 36 |
| 6 | 40 | Holly 44 | 45 |
| 7 | 44 | 47 | 50 |
| 8 | 48 | 51 | 55 |
| 9 | 52 | 58 | 61 |
| 10 | 56 | 60 | 66 |
| 11 | 60 | 65 | 72 |
| 12 | 64 | 69 | 77 |
| 13 | 68 | 74 | 82 |
| 14 | 72 | 78 | 88 |
| 15 | 76 | 83 | 93 |
| 16 | 80 | 87 | 120 |
| 17 | 84 | 92 | |
| 18 | 88 | 98 | |
| 19 | 92 | 101 | |
| 20 | 96 | | |

### did you know?

Dalmatians are famous for their spots. but their puppies are always pure white when they are born. The first black spots usually start to appear when the little ones are three weeks old.

# Too Cute!

The best things come in small packages.

# CHAPTER 3

## The Fash Pack

Does your pooch have a habit of rolling in mud and paddling in ponds? It's time that they were treated to a mutt makeover! Even the hairiest hobo will enjoy being brushed, fussed and pampered.

# Pampered Pooch

All puppies need pampering – as well as making their fur shine, grooming brushes out dirt and old hairs. Fur-bulous!

## Brilliant bonding

Grooming is a great way to get close to your dog. The more your puppy gets used to being touched, hugged and brushed, the more placid, trusting and happy it will be!

## Brushing basics

*1* Spread an old towel on the floor, or if the weather's nice take your puppy outside. Give them lots of fuss so they feel calm and relaxed.

*2* Use a brush first and then a comb to smooth out your puppy's fur. If you come across any knots, gently tease them out. Take care to only brush in the direction that the fur is growing.

*3* Work your way all over your puppy's body, from the head down to the tail. At the beginning, keep the grooming sessions short. Over time you can brush for longer.

# Bathtime Bonkers

Every now and then, your dog is going to need a deep clean. When the weather's nice and your pup is on good form, ask an adult to help you give it a bath.

**Q How often?**

**A** Every two months is more than enough. If you wash your pup too often, you risk washing out the natural oils in its fur.

**Q Inside or outside?**

**A** On a sunny day, outside is always best. It keeps the mess under control! If you have a small dog, however, you might be able to lift it in the bath without too much water being splashed everywhere.

**Q Soap or shampoo?**

**A** Never use soap on your puppy – it could irritate their skin. Use lukewarm water and special dog shampoo. Rinse their fur off afterwards, taking care not to get shampoo in their eyes.

**Q How do I dry my pup?**

**A** Wrap it in a big towel and rub it down so that most of the water is taken away. Keep your pup indoors until its fur dries out completely so it doesn't catch a chill.

**Woofy warning**: some dogs and puppies hate spending time in the tub. See how your pet reacts and get an adult to help you.

# Designer Dawgs

What's the latest pooch couture? Our furry fashion reporter has snapped the very latest looks from the designer dogwalks! Colour in the paw print next to the pup that's working it best.

## Prince prints

A selfie!

## Dexter

Dexter wows in the dinkiest checked shirt EVER!

## Lula

When it comes to leopard print, Lula keeps things classy.

## Maggie

Maggie looks so pretty in pink!

# Fluffy

When it comes to bling,
Fluffy jumps right in!

# Scotty

Scotty's bandana
was flown in from Paris.

# Fifi

Fifi is sitting pretty in
this season's pom-pom
prom dress.

# Mitzy

Mitzy is working
those woollens
so well!

# Riley

Riley's patent
festival boots are
simply to die for!

# Dixie

Dixie has never believed in
'less is more'.

# Let's Accessorise!

Leads, collars and walking coats - when you're a dog there are so many opportunities to look claw-geous! Dig out your pencil case, then use your drawing skills to give these pooches some extra pizzazz!

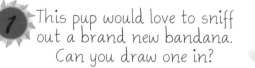

**1** This pup would love to sniff out a brand new bandana. Can you draw one in?

**2** Set off this adorable puppy face with a stunning new hat.

did you know?

In ancient China, wealthy people carried Pekingese puppies around in the sleeves of their robes.

**3** This pooch likes to make a statement. Draw a designer doggy handbag that does just that!

**4** It's a bling thing! Cover this pup in bows, gold and gemstones.

**Woofy warning:**
These doodles are just for fun. It's not safe for real-life doggy divas to wear jewellery. The natural look is best and it's safer, too.

There's a queue of pups at the grooming salon today! Chief pruner, Bella Bouffant, doesn't know who to see first! Help her to organise her bookings by solving this pampered pooch picture quiz.

## Bella Bouffant

1. It's all about the ears with this pup's hair. Is it a...

A. Papillon

B. Poodle

C. Chihuahua

D. Shar Pei ✓

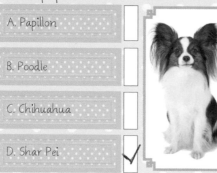

2. This little pup opts for a short back and sides. Is it a...

A. Fox Terrier

B. Miniature Schnauzer

C. King Charles Spaniel

D. Yorkshire Terrier ✓

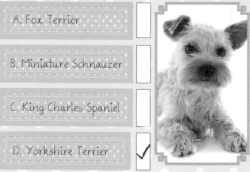

3. This chap keeps things au naturel. Is it a...

A. Border Collie

B. Tibetan Terrier ✓

C. mixed breed

D. Springer Spaniel

4. One of my more outrageous styles! Is it a...

A. Pekingese

B. Tibetan Mastiff

C. Shih Tzu ✓

D. Chinese Crested Dog

5. What a beautiful blonde!
Is it a...

A. Golden Retriever ✓

B. Dalmatian

C. German Shepherd

D. Basset Hound

6. This dog's dreadlocks are
totally fur-bulous! Is it a...

A. Pug

B. Puli

C. Pointer

D. Portuguese Water Dog ✓

7. Guess who takes ages
under the dryer? Is it a...

A. Tibetan Terrier

B. Sussex Spaniel

C. Irish Wolfhound

D. Welsh Corgi ✓

8. This puppy dog's fur is
as soft as velvet. Is it a...

A. Mastiff

B. Irish Setter

C. Whippet ✓

D. Weimaraner

did you know?

Check your answers on page 80.

Bichon Frisé is a French and
Belgian breed. Its name literally
means 'small, curly-haired dog'.
Many people think that poodles
have French origins too, but they
are actually from Germany.

33

# Too Cute!

Well I'm ready. How about you?

# CHAPTER 4

## Doggy Daycare

If you've had a bad day at school or you're feeling down - go and fuss a pup! Doggy pals keep us active, make us giggle and are always up for a game. Who could ask for a better friend?

# Wonderful Walkies

Every dog needs exercise and playtime. Although it can't speak, it will try to tell you this in its own special way. If your pup jumps forward onto its front paws then beats its tail, it's up for fun!

## Out and about

When your mum or dad next pulls on their wellies to go dog-walking, ask to go along, too. Your pooch will love running alongside you in the park, field or beach! As well as keeping your pet fit, walking is a great way to meet new puppy pals and learn social skills.

## Fetch!

Lots of doggies could happily while away their days retrieving toys, slippers and balls. Try throwing a ball with a flinger, then training your pup to wait for your command before running to fetch it again. Remember to give it lots of praise at the end!

### did you know?

If your dog gets warm during an energetic game in the sunshine you may not realise it at first. Hot hounds only sweat through the pads in their feet.

## Water baby?

Some pups can't resist diving into the nearest pond and paddling round in circles. Others are not so sure. Some dogs' body shapes mean that swimming is not possible, especially those with short legs like Dachshunds. Check with an adult before playing in the water with your pet.

## Chew it out

Treat your pet to a rubber toy or a chew bone and they'll have hours of fun! Puppies especially enjoy chewing when their new teeth are coming through as it helps soothe their gums. Don't be surprised if your dog runs off to a favourite hiding spot to chomp.

## Hunt the kong

Kong toys are a great way to entertain your puppy. Fill the hollow with a tasty treat such as peanut butter or cream cheese. Smooth the end off with a knife, then give it to your pet. They'll spend hours chasing the toy, trying to lick the goodies out of the centre!

# Dogs do the Funniest Things

Dogs love to grin, joke and lick your face! Here's twelve of the best hound dog howlers around...

What is the name of the greatest dog detective?

Sherlock Bones!

What did the Dalmatian say when it ate a nice meal?

That hit the spot!

When is a brown dog not a brown dog?

When it is a Greyhound!

What do you call a dog that's come in from the snow?

A slush puppy!

What happens if you cross a Sheepdog with a jelly?

You get the Collie wobbles!

39

# Top Tricks

Some say you can't teach an old dog new tricks, but the opposite is true! If taught patiently and properly, you'll be amazed at the things that your pet can do.

## In a spin

Stand in front of your dog, then hold a treat up for him to see. Say the word "spin" in a gentle, but clear voice, then move the treat to one side so that your dog has to turn his head to follow it. Keep moving the treat round until he has rotated in a complete circle. When he's finished, give him a cuddle and let him eat the treat. Keep practising this and eventually you'll be able to do it without a treat.

did you know...?

Researchers have discovered that most dogs are as clever as a two-year-old child. The brainiest breeds are Border Collies.

## Shake a paw

Sit your dog in front of you. Every time he lifts his paw, say "paw" in a happy voice and give him a tasty treat. Repeat this over and over until he starts to see the connection between your command, the action and the treat. Once he's grasped it, save your treats for the highest lifts, always remembering to give him lots of praise.

## Roll over

Kneel on the floor beside your pup, encouraging him to lie down. Take a tasty treat and hold it next to his nose so that he can sniff it. Now move the treat up and over towards the dog's shoulder, encouraging him to follow the trail with his nose. He should twist further and further until he finally flops over onto his back. Good work! Give him a big cuddle and let him eat the treat. Repeat this over and over, saying the words "roll over!" in a clear voice every time.

### Remember
Pup tricks are just for fun! If your pet seems tired or bored, stop for the day and let them have a rest.

# Too Cute!

Look, it's not going to throw itself.

# CHAPTER 5

Hangin' with me Hound

Does your pet ever look up at you with big, puppy dog eyes that are impossible to resist? Dogs are super-expressive animals - using their tails, bodies and faces to communicate with us and each other.

# Look and Listen

Puppies can't use words, but that doesn't stop them making their feelings known! Look at this picture list, then colour in the paw print next to the moods you've seen your mutt display.

### 1
**I'm feeling fine!**

Body check: mouth open, eyes alert and cheerful, tail wagging behind.

### 2

**Let's take five...**

Body check: both eyes closed, body flat on the ground, legs relaxed.

### 3
**Whatever's happening, count me in!**

Body check: head upright, pricked ears, body tensed and ready to go.

### 4
**Come on guys, let's play!**

Body check: face eager, body crouched forward on front paws, tail wagging.

**5**

*You win!*
Body check: rolled onto back with tummy showing, paws up in front.

**6**

*I'm feeling frightened.*
Body check: cowering body, ears pulled back, tail tucked underneath.

**7**

*Hmm… what's this?*
Body check: walking with nose to ground, eyes alert and focussed, tail upright.

**8**

*Stand back, I'm feeling mad!*
Body check: teeth bared, eyes fixed, hackles up, body ready to pounce.

*did you know?*

When your puppy cocks its leg for the tenth time on a walk it's not bad manners. Going to the toilet is just another way that dogs communicate! Each little deposit is a calling card that other hounds use to sniff out who's been there before.

# Doggy Dictionary

Can you speak dawg? What do your hound's woofs, whimpers and howls really mean? Turn to the doggy dictionary and find out, then learn the best way to tell your pet how much you care.

## Translating from Dog

Barking (flat) ..................................... I'm bored

Barking (high-pitched) ..................... Where are you? I'm worried and upset.

Barking (short and sharp)..................... Raise the alarm, something's going on!

Barking (deep and long) ..................... I'm giving chase.

Growling ..................................... I'm warning you!

Howling..................................... Shout-out to the rest of my pack/help!

Whimpering..................................... Ouch, that hurt.

Whining ..................................... I need food/company/to go outside.

Yawn (one-off)..................................... Hmm... I fancy a rest.

Yawn (repeated)..................................... I'm feeling uneasy about this.

# Puppy pals

Your pet pooch will be your best friend but it's important to know that they're not human – as much as they feel they are!

People love giving hugs to show affection, but puppies aren't always so sure. They are pack animals and so it's very important for them to know who is top dog at all times. If you suddenly hug a dog without getting to know them, they might think you are trying to dominate them. Their first reaction could be to run away or fight back.

If you want to show your pet that you love it, speak in a soft, slow voice (shouting or loud noises can frighten them). Sit sideways on to the pup, avoiding direct eye contact. When they feel calm and relaxed, gently stroke the dog's back.

Your dog can't understand as many sounds as you can, so it keeps a close eye on your body language. When you teach your pup a new command, always come up with a hand gesture to go with it. Having a visual sign to look for will help your pet grasp what you want it to do much more easily.

Puppies are very sensitive. Although they can't understand what you are saying, they pick up on your emotions and feelings. Sometimes you don't need any words to bond with your pet, just being together is enough.

# Four Legged Friends

Ever since dogs were first trained as pets, they have been our devoted companions. What makes them so utterly special? These pages are paws-itively packed full of puppy love!

## Jack London

"A bone to the dog is not charity. Charity is the bone shared with the dog, when you are just as hungry as the dog."

## Mark Twain

"The dog is a gentleman; I hope to go to his heaven not man's."

## Charles de Gaulle

"The better I get to know men, the more I find myself loving dogs."

## Marilyn Monroe

"Dogs never bite me. Just humans."

## Johnny Depp

"The only creatures that are evolved enough to convey pure love are dogs and infants."

## LeAnn Rimes

"My dogs are about unconditional love. It's so wonderful to walk in the door from a long day and all they want to do is be loved and to give and give..."

## Edith Wharton

"My little dog - a heartbeat at my feet."

## Woodrow Wilson

"If a dog will not come to you after having looked you in the face, you should go home and examine your conscience."

## Charles M. Schultz

"Happiness is a warm puppy."

## Unknown

"One reason a dog can be such a comfort when you're feeling blue is that he doesn't try to find out why."

# Famous people pups, too!

- President Obama and his family - Bo and Sunny, Portuguese Water Dogs.
- Ryan Gosling - George, mixed breed.
- Anne Hathaway - Esmeralda, chocolate Labrador.
- Hugh Jackman - Dali, French Bulldog
- The Duke and Duchess of Cambridge - Lupo, black Cocker Spaniel

# Too Cute!

Take that one again. I think I blinked.

# CHAPTER 6

## Superstar Dogs

Puppies were born to perform! The camera loves their adorable faces, funny habits and quirky characters. Many dogs are veterans of stage and screen – some even have their own agents!

# Fluffy and Famous

As well as being the 'it' accessory for A-list celebrities, lots of dogs are stars in their own right! There are a dozen canine characters hiding in this wooftastic wordsearch. Find a pen, then see if you can sniff out each and every one.

| B | K | D | P | M | A | R | T | M | E | J | C |
|---|---|---|---|---|---|---|---|---|---|---|---|
| E | A | F | O | O | D | Y | B | O | O | C | S |
| E | U | G | Y | S | H | X | O | Q | U | I | W |
| T | O | R | W | P | B | N | L | A | D | Y | G |
| H | L | O | Y | A | G | Y | T | Y | P | O | M |
| O | J | M | K | T | D | T | H | Z | T | S | L |
| V | Q | I | N | N | W | Y | Z | O | A | R | B |
| E | E | T | I | V | D | A | T | D | O | L | F |
| N | G | R | L | J | X | Q | K | U | X | C | J |
| T | L | A | S | S | I | E | R | M | P | P | H |
| R | I | N | T | I | N | T | I | N | V | E | H |
| C | H | D | M | J | F | N | V | T | E | K | D |

Look carefully at the letter box. The names could be running in any direction - up, down, diagonally and even back-to-front!

| SCOOBY DOO | | Shaggy's pal and great snack-eater. |
| TRAMP | | A scruffy mutt with a heart of gold. |
| BEETHOVEN | | A giant St Bernard who stars in his own movie franchise. |
| GROMIT | | A Northern pup and Wallace's best friend. |
| DEPUTY DAWG | | A deputy sheriff working at the jailhouse. |
| BOLT | | White American shepherd dog voiced by John Travolta. |
| RIN TIN TIN | | The first Hollywood dog star. |
| HOOCH | | The slobbery hound that drove Turner mad. |
| SLINKY | | Stretchy toy dachshund from *Toy Story*. |
| LASSIE | | An American TV star who always rushed to the rescue. |
| LADY | | Disney's elegant cocker spaniel. |
| TOTO | | The little terrier from *The Wizard of Oz*. |

Check your answers on page 80.

# Doodle Dawgs

Could you be the next 'Andy Warhowl'? Get out your sketchbook and start drawing the puppy you love best.

## You will need

- A photo of your dog
- An HB pencil
- Rubber
- White paper
- Fine black pen
- Pencil sharpener

**1**

The easiest way to get the shape of your pup right is to draw a soft outline first. Study your photo carefully, then draw three circles on the page, set on an imaginary diagonal line. The top circle will be the head, the middle will form the chest and the third marks out the legs.

**2**

With light, soft strokes, add in lines to show where the puppy's snout, legs and tail will be. Don't press hard – you'll want to rub the circles out later.

**3**

Once you've got the basic shape right, use your pencil to link the circles and draw in the outline of your pup. Check back to your photo to make sure that you've got the shape right.

**4**

When you're ready, use the rubber to gently remove the circles inside the outline.

**5**

Draw in your puppy's features. Add the eyes, nose and mouth, then add shape to their ears, paws and tail. Look for details that are unique to your pet. Does it have a fluffy tail or perky ears? Put everything into your picture!

**6**

Use your pencil to shade your puppy's coat. Most dogs have several colours in their fur, so try layering the strokes and using thick and thin strokes to make it look like hair.

**7**

When you've finished shading, use a black fine line pen to draw in whiskers, highlight features and pick out details to add light and shade.

55

# Puppy Dog Tails

We don't just love playing with our pups, we enjoy reading about them, too! Naughty, kind, funny or heroic - books are full of unforgettable hounds! Colour in the paw print next to the magical mutt that is closest to your heart.

## Snowy

'Snowy' in English or 'Milou' in French, dates all the way back to 1929. The little white Wire Fox Terrier is Tintin's sidekick in Hergé's comic book series. Snowy is smart, brave and able to understand humans.

## Nana

Nana is the dog that we'd all love to have around! She is the patient and responsible Newfoundland in J.M. Barrie's *Peter Pan*. In the story, Mr and Mrs Darling hire Nana to care for their three children - Wendy, John and Michael.

## Spot

Eric Hill began the picture book series in 1980 which has now been translated into 60 languages! Spot is a curious yellow puppy, with a spot on his body and a brown-tipped tail.

## Fang

Harry Potter's friend Hagrid is a giant of a man, so no wonder he also has a giant of a dog! Fang is an enormous boarhound (although in the films he's a Neapolitan Mastiff!) with a habit of slobbering all over the place.

The Heffley's new pet dog, Sweetie, first appears in the fourth *Diary of a Wimpy Kid* novel by Jeff Kinney. Greg would have liked to call him 'Ripjaw', or 'Shredder', but his mum opts for a shortened version of 'Sweetheart', even though he is a boy.

## Sweetie

## Timmy

When Enid Blyton created the *Famous Five* series, she wanted a dog to be part of the line-up. Step forward George's faithful pup, Timmy – a loyal mixed breed that loves ice cream, bones and chasing rabbits.

## Pongo and Missus

Everyone knows the *101 Dalmatians* movies, but did you know that the characters come from a book by Dodie Smith? Pongo and his wife Missus are the parents to a litter of 15 puppies and the adopted mum and dad of dozens more.

# Animal Antics

Gnasher, Fred Basset and Snoopy - the world is full of comic strip dogs! Use this space to design your own canine comic strip. Write the words, draw the pictures and fill the speech bubbles.

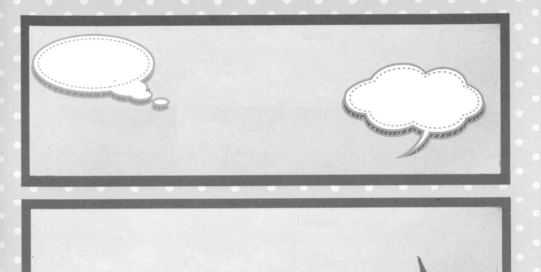

by •••••••••••••••••••••••••••••••

# Too Cute!

Yes, it's very cute. Can you take it back now?

# CHAPTER 7

## It's a Dog's Life!

Let's make every day a doggy day! Make a fur-bulous pet picture frame, circle birthdays on the puppy calendar, pit your wits in a head-scratching hound quiz, then whip up a batch of crunchy treats for your favourite furry friend.

# Fur-bulous Frames

It's time to show the world how much you love your pampered pooch! Make a cute picture frame shaped like a kennel, then pop a picture of your pet inside.

## You will need

- 10 wooden lolly sticks
- A square photo of your puppy (a drawing would work, too)
- Craft glue
- Scissors
- Old newspapers
- Poster paints
- Paintbrush
- Felt-tipped pens or stickers
- A sheet of stiff cardboard
- Pencil
- Ruler
- Sticky tape

**1** Put your photo face-up on a work surface. Arrange four lolly sticks in a square shape on top of it. overlapping the edges to neatly frame the picture. Next take the photo away and put it somewhere safe. then use craft glue to stick the lolly sticks together. This square shape will form the basis of the picture frame.

### Warning
Cutting the lolly sticks can be quite tricky. always ask an adult to help when using scissors.

**2** Find two more lolly sticks and place them at the top of the frame so they create a roof. Glue these in place. too.

**3** Glue extra lolly sticks across the roof of the kennel - you may need to cut some of the sticks down to fit.

**4** Spread out some old newspapers, then get out your paints. Carefully paint the walls and roof of your kennel frame. Use any colours that you like.

**5** When the paint is dry it's time to add some extra decorations. Why not add some stickers or make a sign with your dog's name out of a rectangle of card to go above the door?

Maisy

**6** Now you're ready to mount your pup's picture inside. Put your frame on top of a sheet of stiff cardboard, then trace around the inside square. Using a ruler, draw a square around this that is 1 cm bigger all around.

**7** Following the bigger outline, cut out the cardboard square then carefully stick your picture in the centre of it - make sure it's straight! Now run a line of glue all around the edge of the cardboard and fix it onto the back of the frame.

**8** From the remaining bit of cardboard, cut out a rectangle to make a stand for your kennel frame. Fold over a 1 cm strip at the top of the rectangle and tape this to the back of the picture. Now stand the frame up and let everyone enjoy your masterpiece!

Maisy

# Doggy Days

With this cute canine calendar, you'll never commit another faux-paw again! Use these pages to circle all of your family and friends' birthdays.

## JANUARY

| 1 | 2 | 3 | 4 | 5 | 6 | 7 |
|---|---|---|---|---|---|---|
| 8 | 9 | 10 | 11 | 12 | 13 | 14 |
| 15 | 16 | 17 | 18 | 19 | 20 | 21 |
| 22 | 23 | 24 | 25 | 26 | 27 | 28 |
| 29 | 30 | 31 | | | | |

Sitting pretty in the snow!

## FEBRUARY

| 1 | 2 | 3 | 4 | 5 | 6 | 7 |
|---|---|---|---|---|---|---|
| 8 | 9 | 10 | 11 | 12 | 13 | 14 |
| 15 | 16 | 17 | 18 | 19 | 20 | 21 |
| 22 | 23 | 24 | 25 | 26 | 27 | 28 |
| 29 | | | | | | |

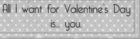

All I want for Valentine's Day is... you.

## MARCH

| 1 | 2 | 3 | 4 | 5 | 6 | 7 |
|---|---|---|---|---|---|---|
| 8 | 9 | 10 | 11 | 12 | 13 | 14 |
| 15 | 16 | 17 | 18 | 19 | 20 | 21 |
| 22 | 23 | 24 | 25 | 26 | 27 | 28 |
| 29 | 30 | 31 | | | | |

It only takes a little sunshine to put a spring in pup's step!

## APRIL

| 1 | 2 | 3 | 4 | 5 | 6 | 7 |
|---|---|---|---|---|---|---|
| 8 | 9 | 10 | 11 | 12 | 13 | 14 |
| 15 | 16 | 17 | 18 | 19 | 20 | 21 |
| 22 | 23 | 24 | 25 | 26 | 27 | 28 |
| 29 | 30 | | | | | |

Fashionable furries can't wait to step out in April showers!

## MAY

| 1 | 2 | 3 | 4 | 5 | 6 | 7 |
|---|---|---|---|---|---|---|
| 8 | 9 | 10 | 11 | 12 | 13 | 14 |
| 15 | 16 | 17 | 18 | 19 | 20 | 21 |
| 22 | 23 | 24 | 25 | 26 | 27 | 28 |
| 29 | 30 | 31 | | | | |

Are you ready for some May madness?

## JUNE

| 1 | 2 | 3 | 4 | 5 | 6 | 7 |
|---|---|---|---|---|---|---|
| 8 | 9 | 10 | 11 | 12 | 13 | 14 |
| 15 | 16 | 17 | 18 | 19 | 20 | 21 |
| 22 | 23 | 24 | 25 | 26 | 27 | 28 |
| 29 | 30 | | | | | |

June days are grrrr-eat for garden games!

## JULY

| 1 | 2 | 3 | 4 | 5 | 6 | 7 |
|---|---|---|---|---|---|---|
| 8 | 9 | 10 | 11 | 12 | 13 | 14 |
| 15 | 16 | 17 | 18 | 19 | 20 | 21 |
| 22 | 23 | 24 | 25 | 26 | 27 | 28 |
| 29 | 30 | 31 | | | | |

School's out - howl for the holidays!

## AUGUST

| 1 | 2 | 3 | 4 | 5 | 6 | 7 |
|---|---|---|---|---|---|---|
| 8 | 9 | 10 | 11 | 12 | 13 | 14 |
| 15 | 16 | 17 | 18 | 19 | 20 | 21 |
| 22 | 23 | 24 | 25 | 26 | 27 | 28 |
| 29 | 30 | 31 | | | | |

Hot dogs stretch out in the summer sun.

## SEPTEMBER

| 1 | 2 | 3 | 4 | 5 | 6 | 7 |
|---|---|---|---|---|---|---|
| 8 | 9 | 10 | 11 | 12 | 13 | 14 |
| 15 | 16 | 17 | 18 | 19 | 20 | 21 |
| 22 | 23 | 24 | 25 | 26 | 27 | 28 |
| 29 | 30 | | | | | |

Autumn is twice as nice when you snuggle up with a friend.

## OCTOBER

| 1 | 2 | 3 | 4 | 5 | 6 | 7 |
|---|---|---|---|---|---|---|
| 8 | 9 | 10 | 11 | 12 | 13 | 14 |
| 15 | 16 | 17 | 18 | 19 | 20 | 21 |
| 22 | 23 | 24 | 25 | 26 | 27 | 28 |
| 29 | 30 | 31 | | | | |

Hound dogs come out to share the Halloween fun!

## NOVEMBER

| 1 | 2 | 3 | 4 | 5 | 6 | 7 |
|---|---|---|---|---|---|---|
| 8 | 9 | 10 | 11 | 12 | 13 | 14 |
| 15 | 16 | 17 | 18 | 19 | 20 | 21 |
| 22 | 23 | 24 | 25 | 26 | 27 | 28 |
| 29 | 30 | | | | | |

In November, there's a puppy on every pavement.

## DECEMBER

| 1 | 2 | 3 | 4 | 5 | 6 | 7 |
|---|---|---|---|---|---|---|
| 8 | 9 | 10 | 11 | 12 | 13 | 14 |
| 15 | 16 | 17 | 18 | 19 | 20 | 21 |
| 22 | 23 | 24 | 25 | 26 | 27 | 28 |
| 29 | 30 | 31 | | | | |

May all your waggy Christmas wishes come true...

## did you know?

Some smart stray dogs in Russia have worked out how to ride on underground trains! They travel from station to station, to find the busiest parts of the city. They've learned that these are the places where they're most likely to find food.

# Take a Bite

Have you been sat up and paying attention so far? Let's find out! Get your dog's tail wagging by trying your luck at this puzzling puppy quiz. Grab a pen and tick the right answers.

1. Which dog is the fastest on four legs?

A. the Spaniel

B. the Greyhound

C. the German Shepherd

D. the Bull Terrier

2. Which of these foods is not dangerous to dogs?

A. chocolate

B. pasta

C. raisins

D. onions

3. Why do pups get so attached to their owners?

A. they see them as part of their pack

B. they like their smell

C. they think they are their mum or dad

D. because owners feed them

4. At what age can a female dog start having babies?

A. three years old

B. at least six months old

C. anytime

D. after its first birthday

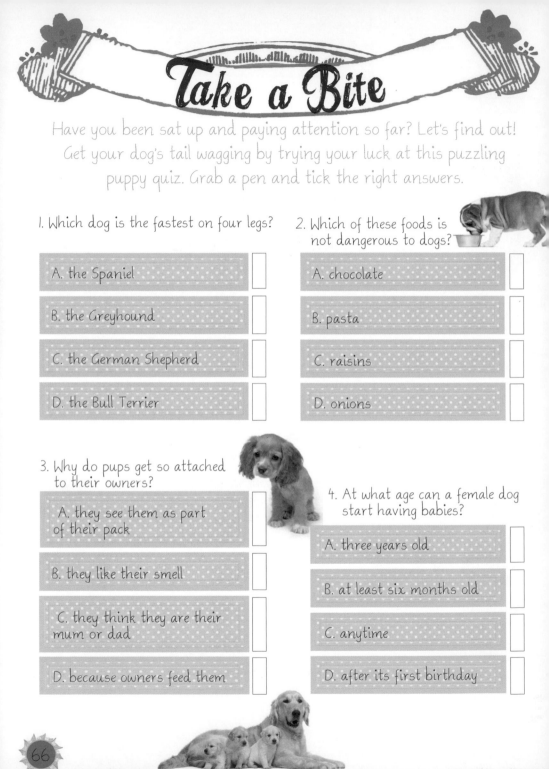

5. Where's the best place to pat a dog you don't know very well?

A. on the head

B. on the tummy

C. on the face

D. on the shoulders

6. How many breeds of dog are there?

A. around 250

B. around 300

C. around 400

D. around 550

7. Why do puppies chew everything?

A. they're naturally cheeky

B. it helps digest their food

C. it soothes their gums during teething

D. it is just a habit

8. What animal are all dogs descended from?

A. the grey wolf

B. the jackal

C. the coyote

D. the hyena

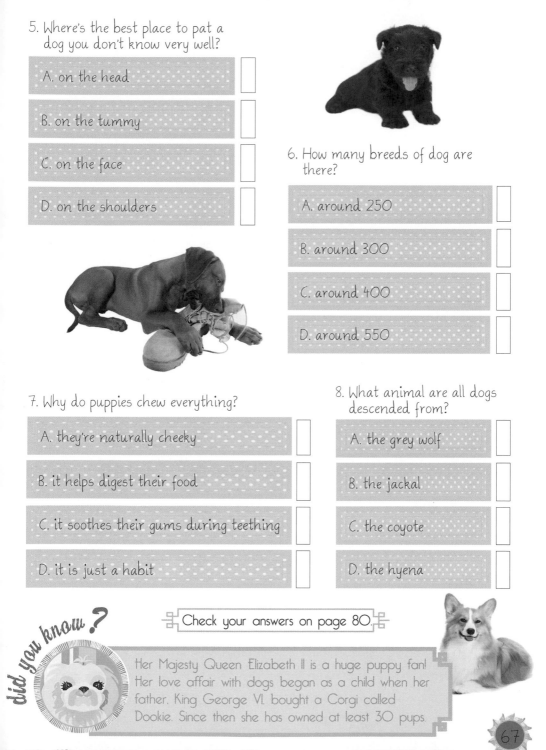

did you know?

Check your answers on page 80.

Her Majesty Queen Elizabeth II is a huge puppy fan! Her love affair with dogs began as a child when her father, King George VI, bought a Corgi called Dookie. Since then she has owned at least 30 pups.

# Dribbly and Delicious

Want to win your pup's heart forever? Make them a gourmet batch of doggy treats! This scrummy pet recipe will have your hound howling for more every time you get cooking.

## You will need

- A little olive oil for greasing
- 250g unsalted peanut butter
- 250ml skimmed milk
- 250g wholewheat flour
- 1 tablespoon baking powder
- Cookie cutter

**Makes 24 doggy bites**

**1** Preheat the oven to 190°C/375°F/Gas Mark 4. Dip some kitchen towel in a little olive oil. then grease a flat baking tray.

**2** Tip the peanut butter into a mixing bowl. then use a wooden spoon to stir in the milk. In another bowl. blend the flour and baking powder together.

**3** Tip some of the flour mixture into the peanut butter and milk. Beat it in. then gradually add more and more until everything is combined. The ingredients will form a moist. nutty dough.

**4** Sprinkle some flour onto a clean worktop, then knead the dough until it's soft. Roll it flat with a rolling pin, turning it regularly so that it doesn't stick.

**5** Use cookie cutters to press biscuit shapes out of the dough. You could press out hearts, stars or even bones. Put each doggy bite onto the baking tray.

**6** Pop the doggy bites into the oven to bake. This should take around 15 minutes. When they're ready, the treats will have turned a warm golden brown. Leave the bites to cool fully before feeding one to your lucky pup!

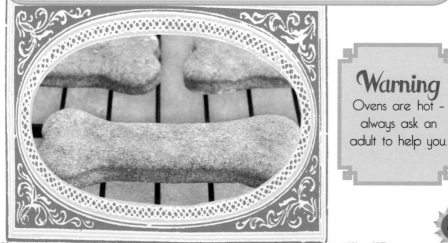

# Too Cute!

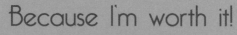

Because I'm worth it!

# CHAPTER 8

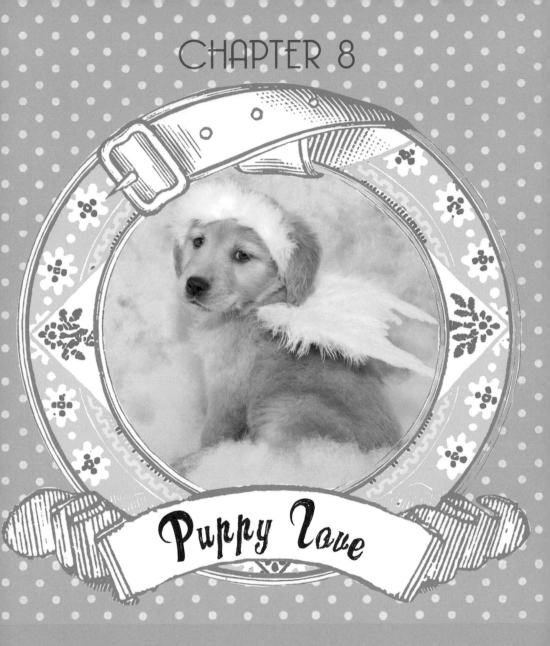

## Puppy Love

When it comes to sweet gestures, no one can outdo a doggy.
Who else would greet you with a slurpy hello lick, run around in
excited circles and thump its tail at the very mention of going out
together? Aww… it really is a case of puppy love!

# My Puppy Pal

These are your very own puppy pages! Write about your special pet, it could be a real dog or a pooch you'd love to play with.

Name: ..........................

Boy or Girl: ..................

Age: ..............................

Fur colour: ..................

Eye colour: ...................

Stick a picture of your puppy pal here.

Unusual markings: ...............................................................

.........................................................................................

.........................................................................................

The things they do that make me laugh: .......................................

.........................................................................................

.........................................................................................

.........................................................................................

.........................................................................................

Breed: ...................................

Favourite toy: .........................

Favourite food: .........................

Five words to describe my puppy:
1 ...........................................
2 ...........................................
3 ...........................................
4 ...........................................
5 ...........................................

What makes my puppy special: ...........................................
...........................................................................
...........................................................................

Draw a picture of your puppy pal here.

A Why do a job that someone else could do for you?

B Things are the wrong way round. Something small is in charge of something much too important.

C I'm heading off, but I don't want to tell you where I'm going.

D I'm completely thrilled!

E It's much wiser to let things be.

F Your time will come.

G After a while it is too late to change the way someone does something.

H This joke takes ages to tell, but the ending is daft.

Check your answers on page 80.

# Utterly Adorable!

This photo album is packed full of puppy pics! Look at each delectable doggy snap, then think up a caption to write underneath it. The first picture has been labelled to get you started.

Because pets love
selfies, too!

did you know ?

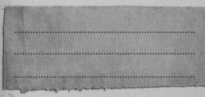

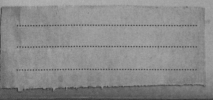

# In The Dog House

Every dog needs somewhere comfy to curl up at the end of the day. Use these pages to sketch your own designer kennel. Outline the shape of the doggy den, decorate the walls then sketch what it's like inside. When you've drawn your puppy paradise, colour it in. Night, night puppy dog!

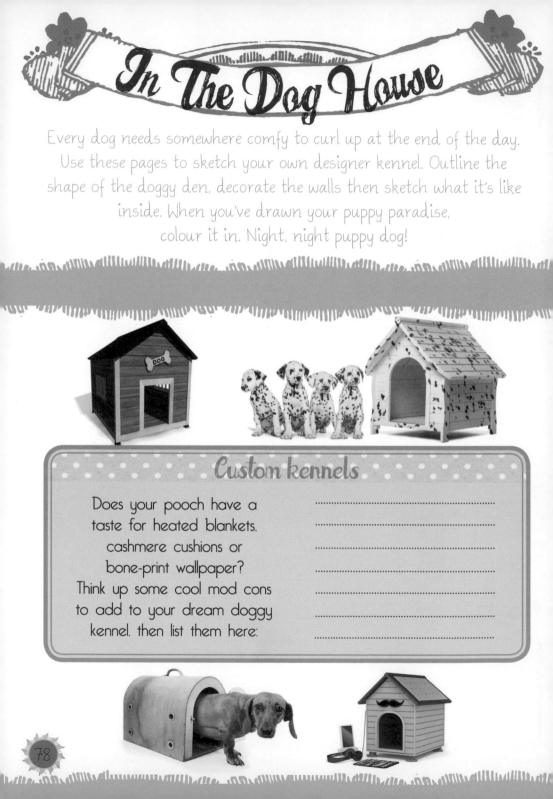

## Custom kennels

Does your pooch have a taste for heated blankets, cashmere cushions or bone-print wallpaper? Think up some cool mod cons to add to your dream doggy kennel. then list them here:

...............................................
...............................................
...............................................
...............................................
...............................................
...............................................
...............................................

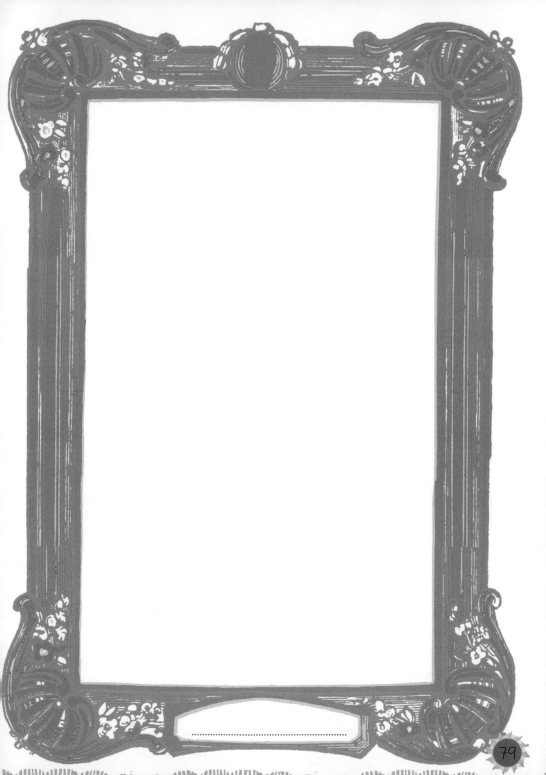

# Answers

## Pages 10-11
### Magical Mix-ups
1. E
2. F
3. D
4. C
5. A
6. B

## Pages 32-33
### Picture This
1. A
2. D
3. C
4. D
5. A
6. B
7. A
8. D

## Pages 52-53
### Fluffy and Famous

## Pages 66-67
### Take a Bite!
1. B
2. B
3. A
4. B
5. D
6. C
7. C
8. A

## Pages 74-75
### Woofy Words
1. H
2. E
3. B
4. G
5. D
6. F
7. A
8. C

THE END
WOOF!